Diamond Dazzle

by Sam Gayton
Illustrated by Emma Levey

OXFORD
UNIVERSITY PRESS

In this story …

Pip and Kit run *Finders Squeakers* – a lost and found agency. They help return lost things to their owners.

The Daily Newts

The Big Dazzle is missing!

Report by: Sal Mander

Last night, The Big Dazzle – the world's largest diamond – was stolen from its display case at the Tailton Museum. Police detective Ella Mentry told reporters, "The Big Dazzle is <u>rare</u>. It's worth a fortune. We won't stop until we find it." The detective also said that a black-and-white feather was found by the display case. "Fowl play is suspected," she added.

The Big Dazzle

The scene of the crime

Continued on page 4 …

The Big Dazzle is a <u>rare</u> diamond. Does this mean that there are lots of diamonds like The Big Dazzle or hardly any?

Chapter 1
The missing invention

Kit looked up from the newspaper. "Let's find that diamond, Pip!" he said. "Things have been quiet recently and I've got itchy paws."

"It says here that the police are already looking for it," Pip said, glancing at the paper.

Just then, the screen behind them went *ping*!

Pip swivelled in her chair and read the email.

"Never mind The Big Dazzle, Kit," said Pip. "It looks like we might have a case of our own."

"What's missing?" Kit asked. "Stolen sapphires? A pilfered pearl?"

Pip shook her head. "Something much more interesting …"

Dear Finders Squeakers,

I need your help to find my missing invention: the Obey Ray. It's a hypnosis machine. I made it to help train my pet ferret, Fergus, to do as he's told and stop being so naughty. However, it disappeared from my laboratory two nights ago. The only thing left behind by the thief was a single black-and-white feather.

From
Doctor Kruft

Kit gasped. "Doctor Kruft's laboratory is near the museum where The Big Dazzle was stolen. The two crimes might be linked!"

Pip nodded. "Bird feathers were found in both places too …"

"I bet it's that dastardly pigeon, Coo!" Kit scowled. "He promised us that he would never steal again!"

Pip stroked her whiskers. "Coo's feathers are grey, not black and white. We need to investigate."

Looking at the photo Doctor Kruft had sent, Pip smiled. "Do you speak ferret, Kit?"

"Of course!" said Kit. "Why?"

Pip was already heading for their motorbike. She signalled to Kit to follow her. "Maybe Fergus the ferret saw what happened. Come on!"

Pip signalled to Kit to follow her. What sort of signal might she have used?

Chapter 2
The naughtiest pet in Tailton

Doctor Kruft's laboratory was a tall brick and glass <u>structure</u>. Pip and Kit drove down a side alleyway. They got off their bike and hopped up on to a window ledge.

"What a mess!" Kit whispered.

Pip nodded. The laboratory was full of half-finished machines. Tools and plans for inventions were scattered about.

What word could you use instead of '<u>structure</u>' to describe Doctor Kruft's laboratory?

Doctor Kruft was at her workbench. Through the open window, Pip could hear her muffled cries. "Oh no, Fergus! Not again!"

The doctor's pet ferret was on the table being naughty. Very, *very* naughty. As Pip and Kit watched, Fergus nibbled through some wires, tipped over a microscope and pulled all the lettuce from the doctor's sandwich.

Kit frowned. "I can see why the doctor invented the Obey Ray."

"We better get it back to her as soon as possible," agreed Pip.

The doctor looked at her ruined sandwich. "I will have to go to a cafe for lunch," she told Fergus. "Please *try* to behave while I'm out."

As the doctor left, Pip and Kit slipped through the open window.

"Excuse me, Fergus," Kit said to the ferret. "We'd like to ask you a few questions."

Fergus was treading tomato-sauce paw prints all over the desk. "Who are you?" he asked rudely, before darting down to the floor to nibble on one of the doctor's shoes.

"We're from *Finders Squeakers*," Kit answered. "We're trying to find the doctor's missing Obey Ray."

"Oh, *that* thing," said Fergus, as he hid some car keys under the desk. "Yeah, some bird came through the window yesterday and flew off with it in its claws."

"Aha!" said Kit. "It has to be Coo."

Pip frowned. "What type of bird was it, Fergus? A pigeon?"

Fergus yawned and tipped over a bin. "*I don't know*," he said. "I'm not a bird expert."

"You aren't being very helpful," Pip said, folding her arms. "If you carry on like this, the doctor will have to take you to ferret training classes."

Fergus stopped what he was doing and gulped. "Ferret training classes?" he said anxiously. "That doesn't sound much fun."

"Come on, Pip," said Kit. "Let's see if Coo is available to answer some questions."

As they left, Fergus looked guiltily at all the mess he'd made. "Perhaps I should start behaving a little better," he muttered to himself.

Kit wanted to see if Coo was available to answer some questions. What did he mean by this?

Chapter 3
The secret attic

Back on their motorbike, Pip and Kit raced towards Coo's nest. It was empty.

"Let's look up there," Pip said, nodding at a deserted house next to Coo's tree. "I got a tip-off from a friendly seagull that Coo keeps his disguises in that attic."

"I'll bring the Catcher 3000," Kit said, hauling a metal grabber from the sidecar. "Just in case."

They tiptoed up to the attic, wincing with every creak of the staircase. Pip's ears began to tingle in anticipation.

When they reached the top step, they paused outside the door.

Kit held up the Catcher 3000 and whispered, "One, two, three …"

Pip and Kit burst into the attic. Soft, downy feathers flew up into the air as they threw the door open. Disguises lay strewn across the floor, covered in birdseed. There were two mirrors, one large and one small, propped up in the corner. In the centre of the room stood Coo, staring at them with large, unblinking eyes.

Something huge glittered beside him, like a star that had fallen from the sky.

"The Big Dazzle!" said Kit.

"Hold it there, Coo!" Pip yelled. "Don't try to escape!"

Coo continued staring at Pip and Kit, as if he were a statue.

"Hello?" Stepping closer, Kit waved a paw in front of the pigeon's face. "Coo?"

Kit seized the diamond with the Catcher 3000. Coo still didn't move.

"I stole the diamond," the pigeon said suddenly. His voice was slow and dreamy. "I stole the diamond. The Mighty Coo, and no one else."

Pip frowned. "Something strange is going on," she said to Kit.

"I stole the diamond," Coo said again. "It was me …"

Kit seized the diamond. What does the word 'seize' tell us about the way Kit got the diamond?

"Coo!" Kit gently tapped the pigeon on the wing. "It's as if he isn't really *awake*."

At once, it was like a light had been switched on in Coo's head. He blinked, gave a squawk and flapped his wings in panic.

"What's going on?" he cried, his head bobbing up and down. "Pip Squeak? Kit Bags? Why are you here?"

"Where did you get this, Coo?" Kit asked sternly, holding up The Big Dazzle.

Coo's eyes widened in shock as he spotted the diamond. "I … I … thought that was a dream," he protested. "I didn't think I'd actually stolen it! Please, you have to believe me. I'm a changed pigeon!"

Pip didn't know what to do. She had caught Coo stealing things before, but he had never acted quite like this. He seemed really upset.

"Just tell us the truth, Coo," she said. "What happened?"

Coo sniffed. "The last thing I remember is a swirling disc. I couldn't help looking at it."

Kit gasped. "Pip, could that be the Obey Ray?" he wondered.

Pip nodded. "Coo, it sounds like someone used an invention called the Obey Ray to hypnotize you," Pip explained. "Who would do such a thing?"

"That would be telling," said a voice behind them.

Chapter 4
The villain revealed

At the entrance to the attic, another bird had appeared. She had black-and-white feathers, with vivid streaks of blue and emerald green in her tail. She was holding Doctor Kruft's Obey Ray in her wings. The swirling hypno-disc was spinning round and round. Pip couldn't look away. It was like a whirlpool, sucking her in …

"Close your eyes!" Pip cried, but her eyelids weren't working. Coo and Kit were both staring open-mouthed at the Obey Ray's hypno-disc. They had fallen under its power.

With the last of her strength, Pip took a step backwards. Her foot slipped on some birdseed, and she collapsed in a heap. At once, she had broken the Obey Ray's hold over her.

"Who are you?" Pip cried, glaring at the mysterious bird.

"I'm Maggie Pie," the bird said, keeping the Obey Ray trained on Kit and Coo. "You must be Pip Squeak. I've read about you in *The Daily Newts*. You're rather famous. I, on the other hand, like to keep out of the newspapers."

"You like others to take the blame for your crimes, you mean," said Pip.

Maggie Pie cawed with laughter. "That's why I'll never get caught," she said. "With the Obey Ray, I can hypnotize whomever I like, and I can make them take the blame for things *I've* stolen."

"Like with Coo and The Big Dazzle," said Pip.

"Exactly," said Maggie, cackling. In one swift move, she aimed the Obey Ray straight at Pip.

Pip quickly turned her head away from the Obey Ray's hypno-disc. "I'm going to let everyone know what a bad magpie you are," she told Maggie. "I'll tell the police, and I'll tell Sal at *The Daily Newts*."

Maggie cocked her head. Her beak twisted into a mocking smile. "Oh no, you won't," she said. Her voice was soft with menace.

Pip kept her head turned away from Maggie. "If I don't look at the Obey Ray, you can't stop me!"

Maggie cawed again. Her dark beady eyes shone. "I'm not going to stop you," she said. "Kit is. Aren't you, Kit?"

"Yes, Maggie," said Kit, hypnotized. "Whatever you say."

Before Pip could react, Kit dropped the Catcher 3000 with a clang. He lurched towards Pip and wrapped his tail around her like a furry rope. Pip was trapped!

"Kit!" she cried, desperately. "Let me go! Snap out of it!"

However, Kit's face remained blank.

"Even friendship cannot stand in the way of the Obey Ray!" Maggie cackled.

Pip's mind raced. She had to get through to Kit. How had Coo's hypnosis been broken? First, Kit had tapped Coo on the wing. After that, he had said something. What was it?

Suddenly, Pip remembered.

"*Awake!*" she cried.

Coo and Kit both blinked and looked around in confusion.

"Huh?" Kit unwrapped his tail and Pip scrabbled free. "What's going on?" Kit asked, rubbing his eyes.

With a furious screech, Maggie Pie swung the swirling Obey Ray towards them all again.

Why do you think Maggie Pie was furious?

Kit and Coo froze like statues. They were hypnotized again! Pip rolled sideways and grabbed the Catcher 3000. It was almost too heavy for her to lift, but she managed to aim it and push the button.

   WHOOSH! The Catcher 3000 sprang out and grabbed Coo's mirror. As Maggie turned the Obey Ray towards Pip once more, Pip swung the mirror towards Maggie.

"No!" Maggie cried, as she saw the Obey Ray's swirling hypno-disc reflected in the mirror. "I can't ... look ... away ..."

<u>Gradually</u>, she trailed off into silence. Pip sat gasping for breath in the middle of the attic. It was over.

If Maggie stopped talking <u>gradually</u>, how did she do it? Can you say, "I can't ... look ... away..." as Maggie did?

Chapter 5
The final dilemma

"Maggie?" Pip said. "Turn off the Obey Ray, please, and then bring it over here to me."

"Yes, Pip Squeak," said Maggie, obediently.

Pip put The Big Dazzle safely away in her backpack and took the batteries out of the Obey Ray. "All of you, AWAKE!" she yelled.

"My head …" Maggie groaned.

"What just happened?" Coo said, sleepily.

Kit looked at his tail in a daze. "Did I trap you, Pip? I'm so sorry!"

Pip shook her head. "If anyone should say sorry, it's Maggie Pie."

Maggie scowled. "Never!" She turned and flew straight towards the window. In a flurry of black-and-white feathers, she was gone.

"Don't worry," Pip told Kit. "She won't get away with it. We're going to tell the whole story to Sal so that she can report it in *The Daily Newts*. From now on, Maggie Pie will have to pay the price for her actions."

"Good," said Coo, ruffling his feathers. "Maybe she'll change her ways, just like I did."

Pip grinned. "Exactly. Now, Coo, you need to come with us. We've got a diamond to return!"

The Daily Newts

Thank-Coo Very Much

Report by: Sal Mander

The former robber, Coo Lightfeathers, astounded police when he helped return the missing diamond, The Big Dazzle, to Tailton Museum. The pigeon said, "I'm a changed bird. It's much nicer grabbing the headlines for being a hero instead of a villain." The suspect, Maggie Pie, is still at large.

Continued on page 2 …

Hero, Coo Lightfeathers

Wanted, Maggie Pie
If you see this bird, contact the police immediately.

The next day …

Pip and Kit arrived outside Doctor Kruft's laboratory. Even though they had saved the day and found the Obey Ray, Pip felt anxious. Kit was nibbling his paws, and she guessed he felt the same.

"You're thinking about the Obey Ray, aren't you?" she asked.

Kit sighed. "It's a dangerous invention."

"It's not right to hypnotize anyone without their permission," Pip agreed.

"What if the Obey Ray falls into the wrong hands again?" Kit replied. "Do you think we should keep it instead?"

"Shh! Listen," said Pip. "Do you hear that?"

Kit's ears pricked up. From inside the laboratory, they could hear Doctor Kruft applauding.

"Well done, Fergus!" she was saying. "What a good ferret!"

Pip and Kit peered through the laboratory window. They were <u>astonished</u> by what they saw.

"There's no mess," said Pip.

"Or paw prints," added Kit.

"He hasn't nibbled a single one of the doctor's books," said Pip. "He's changed!"

Why were Pip and Kit <u>astonished</u>? Can you read the page again in an <u>astonished</u> voice?

"I've changed my mind about the Obey Ray," Doctor Kruft said to Fergus. "After it went missing, I was planning to take you to ferret training classes. However, you've been so well-behaved since then that I don't need to … And I don't need that silly invention, either."

"If I ever get the Obey Ray back, Fergus," continued Doctor Kruft, "I'll take it apart and use the bits for spares!"

Pip and Kit looked at each other and grinned. Then they hopped down from the window ledge and left the Obey Ray on the doorstep for the doctor to find.

After that, they got on their motorbike and headed home for a well-earned biscuit.

Read and discuss

Read and talk about the following questions.

Page 3: Can you think of something else that is rare, apart from diamonds?

Page 8: Pip signalled to Kit to follow her. What types of signals do we use to communicate 'yes' and 'no' without talking?

Page 9: Two structures are mentioned on this page. What are they?

Page 15: What time of day is food available at your school?'

Page 20: Can you think of another word to use instead of 'seize'?

Page 33: Have you ever felt furious? Why? What happened?

Page 36: Can you think of something that happens gradually?

Page 45: Can you make an astonished face?